American Indians of the East
Woodland People

Heather E. Schwartz

Consultants

Katie Blomquist, M.Ed.
Fairfax County Public Schools

Nicholas Baker, Ed.D.
Supervisor of Curriculum and Instruction
Colonial School District, DE

Vanessa Ann Gunther, Ph.D.
Department of History
Chapman University

Publishing Credits

Rachelle Cracchiolo, M.S.Ed., *Publisher*
Conni Medina, M.A.Ed., *Managing Editor*
Emily R. Smith, M.A.Ed., *Series Developer*
Diana Kenney, M.A.Ed., NBCT, *Content Director*
Johnson Nguyen, *Multimedia Designer*
Lynette Ordoñez, *Editor*

Image Credits: Cover and p. 1 Collection of the New-York Historical Society, USA/Bridgeman Images; pp. 2-3, 4–5, 8, 10–11, 11, 12–13, 14–15, 18, 19, 20, 22, 31, back cover North Wind Picture Archives; pp. 7, 16 NativeStock/North Wind Picture Archives; pp. 16, 17, 21, 24–25 Granger, NYC; p. 21 Pictorial Press Ltd/Alamy; p. 23 LOC [LC-DIG-ds-03379]; p. 26 Sogospelman/Wikimedia Commons; pp. 27, 32 Rick Maiman/Polaris/Newscom; all other images from iStock and/or Shutterstock.

Library of Congress Cataloging-in-Publication Data

Names: Schwartz, Heather E., author.
Title: American indians of the East : woodland people / Heather E. Schwartz.
Description: Huntington Beach, CA : Teacher Created Materials, 2017. | Includes index.
Identifiers: LCCN 2015051136 (print) | LCCN 2016000148 (ebook) | ISBN 9781493830718 (pbk.) | ISBN 9781480756731 (eBook)
Subjects: LCSH: Indians of North America--East (U.S.)--History--Juvenile literature.
Classification; LCC E78.E2 S39 2017 (print) | LCC E78.E2 (ebook) | DDC 970.004/97--dc23
LC record available at http://lccn.loc.gov/2015051136

Teacher Created Materials

5301 Oceanus Drive
Huntington Beach, CA 92649-1030
http://www.tcmpub.com
ISBN 978-1-4938-3071-8

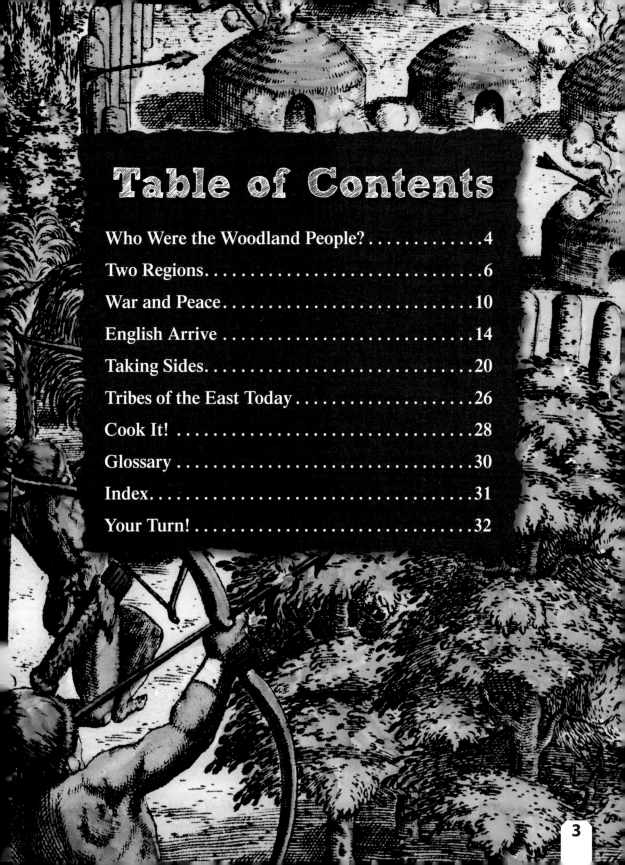

Table of Contents

Who Were the Woodland People?

Long ago, American Indian **tribes** stretched across the East. They were diverse groups with different languages and **customs**. But they had a shared history.

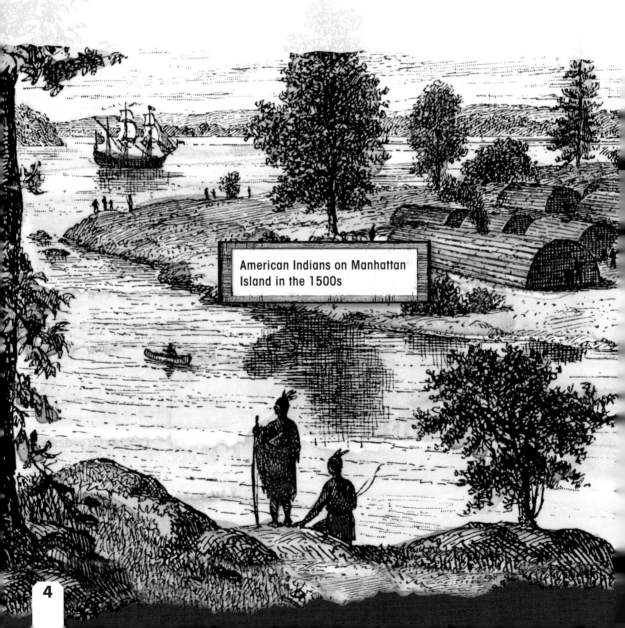

American Indians on Manhattan Island in the 1500s

These tribes lived between the Atlantic Ocean and the Mississippi River. Since the tribes lived mostly in forests, they are called the Woodland People.

The Woodland People lived well for centuries. They used the land for food and other resources. Some tribes formed **alliances**. Some traded with each other. Their **cultures** thrived.

But everything changed when English settlers arrived. They wanted land that belonged to the Woodland People. It became difficult for the settlers and the tribes to get along. Life would never be the same.

What's in a Name?

Christopher Columbus landed in the Caribbean in 1492. He thought he had landed in India. So, he called the people he saw *Indians*.

Two Regions

The Woodland People lived in various parts of eastern North America. They spoke many languages, including Iroquoian (eer-uh-KWOY-uhn) and Algonquian (al-GAHN-kwuhn). Cultures varied between northeastern and southeastern tribes. One major reason for this was the different climates of the regions.

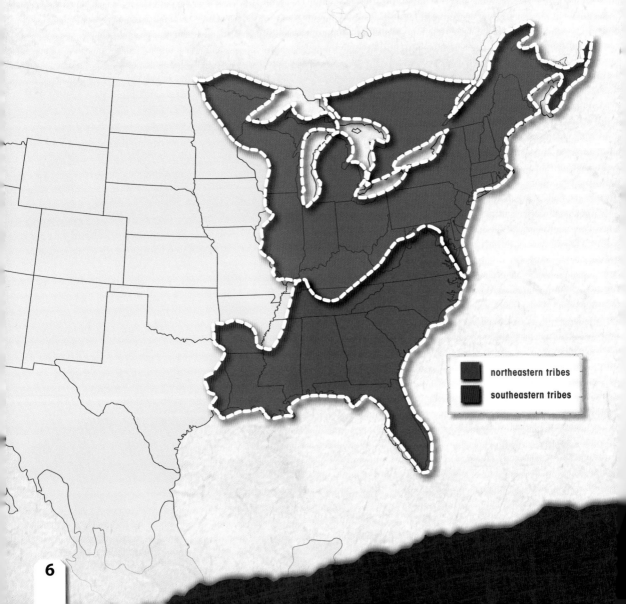

northeastern tribes

southeastern tribes

a wigwam and a longhouse

Northeastern Tribes

Among others, the tribes of the Northeast included the Seneca, Mohawk, Mohican, Oneida, and Shawnee. The climate in the Northeast is cooler than in the Southeast. People needed to protect their bodies from the cold. So they wore clothes made of deerskin to keep warm.

Northeastern tribes hunted deer, rabbit, bison, bear, and other animals. They also farmed. They grew corn, beans, and squash.

People in northeastern tribes lived in wigwams and longhouses. Wigwams were made of sheets of bark that were placed on top of a wooden frame. Longhouses were framed with wooden posts and poles. They were held together with rope or strips of bark. Then, they were covered in bark. Many families lived together in a longhouse. These homes helped them survive harsh winters.

Three Sisters

Corn, beans, and squash are known as the Three Sisters. They grow well together. Squash leaves kept the soil moist. Beans grow up the corn stalks. The beans also keep the soil fertile.

Southeastern Tribes

Some of the southeastern tribes included the Cherokee, Chickasaw, Choctaw, Creek, and Natchez. The climate of the Southeast is warmer than the Northeast. So people in southeastern tribes did not wear as much clothing as the people in northeastern tribes. When it was cold, they wore clothing made of woven bark and moss.

Southeastern tribes had a strong farming culture. This was because the soil is especially good for growing crops. Like the northeastern tribes, they grew corn, beans, and squash.

Southeastern tribes lived mainly in **wattle and daub** houses. Frames were woven out of wood, rivercane, and vines. The frames were then covered in a clay mixture. Roofs were made of thatched grass or bark. Some tribes also lived in thatched grass houses. They were supported by poles and covered in grass. These houses were ideal for the warmer southeastern climate.

Mound Builders

Long ago, some Woodland People built mounds. These large mounds often marked burial sites.

Etowah Indian Mound in Georgia

wattle and daub house

War and Peace

Eastern tribes often had peaceful relations with one another. But sometimes, they clashed violently. Some waged war or had ongoing feuds.

When tribes attacked each other, it was often by **ambush**, or surprise attack. A large group hid in trees and bushes. Then, they split up in smaller groups and attacked.

A tribe waits to ambush an enemy.

The Woodland People had a specific reason for this ambush tactic. They had a shared spiritual belief that the souls of people killed in battle would not rest after death. Most battles that began with a surprise attack ended quickly and fewer of their own lives were lost.

Before attacks were carried out, there were many steps to follow. Women of the tribe chose a war chief. The war chief formed an attacking party. Then, he had to get village approval. He held a **ceremonial** feast. Finally, he led his party in the attack.

Weapons and Armor

The Woodland People wielded clubs, spears, stone-tipped axes, and stone-tipped arrows. They protected themselves with bark shields and wooden armor.

The Woodland People did not care about gaining enemy land. Tribes had other reasons for attacking. Tribes often attacked for revenge. Or they attacked to give young men a chance to prove their skills as warriors. Sometimes, young men attacked without village approval. They were eager to show off their skills and to gain respect. But their unapproved attacks often ended peace agreements.

Tribes also attacked to steal members of other tribes. **Captives** sometimes replaced deceased members of the tribe. This was often the case with women and children. The children were adopted into new families. They were given new names. Male captives were often tortured for a few days. Then, they were put to death. Other times, they became slaves of the people who captured them.

American Indians attack an enemy village.

English Arrive

Conflict took on a new meaning in the 17th century. That's when English **colonists** began to arrive. The first settlers came to the Virginia area in 1607. They hoped to claim land for England and prosper from the land. They also wanted to change native culture. They thought the Woodland People were **savages**. They wanted to **convert** them to **Christianity**.

The settlers built a **colony** called Jamestown. Some tribes lived near Jamestown. Many of these tribes were from the Powhatan Chiefdom. This was a group of tribes that had formed an alliance. The English claimed that the land was theirs. But the land was already the home of thousands of people.

The tribes reacted quickly. They attacked Jamestown. But soon, their attitude changed. The colonists did not appear powerful. They did not seem like a group that would threaten the Powhatan way of life. And, the tribes wanted to trade for English weapons.

The leader of the Powhatan Chiefdom made peace with the colonists. He accepted them and began to treat them as friends.

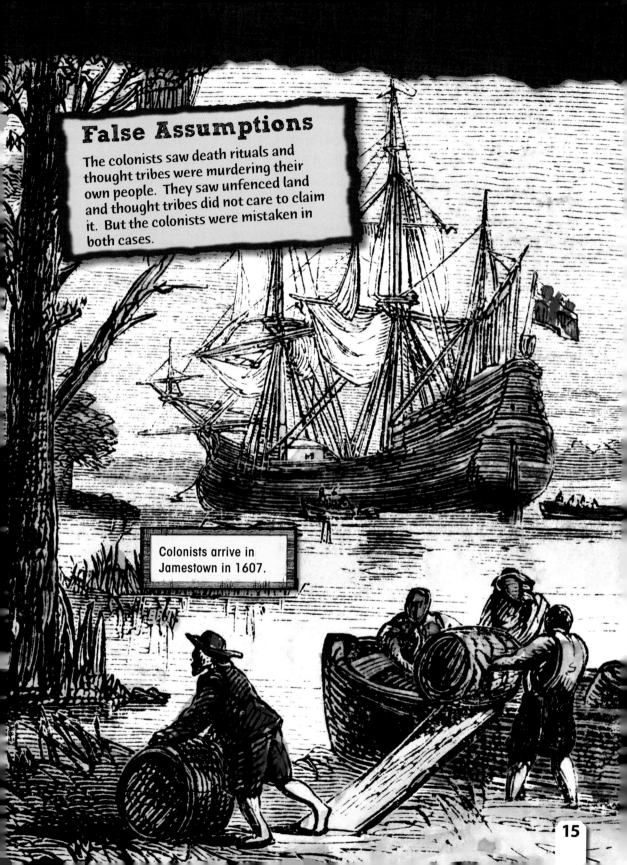

False Assumptions

The colonists saw death rituals and thought tribes were murdering their own people. They saw unfenced land and thought tribes did not care to claim it. But the colonists were mistaken in both cases.

Colonists arrive in Jamestown in 1607.

The Powhatans began trading with colonists. Colonists gave the Powhatans copper and coins. They also gave them **manufactured** goods from Europe, such as kettles, beads, and metal tools. In return, the Powhatans gave colonists pearls, fur, and beaver hats. But most importantly, they gave colonists food. The colonists had little food of their own. They traded almost everything they had for food. And the Powhatans wanted more supplies. They grew to depend on each other.

Pocahontas

Pocahontas was the daughter of the Powhatan leader. She brought food to Jamestown and convinced the English to release Powhatan prisoners.

metal cooking pot

But the colonists and the Powhatans had different views about the land. Colonists wanted to own it. They wanted to **profit** from the land. They hoped to find gold. But the Powhatans thought that the land should be preserved. The colonists and the Powhatans could not agree. Tension between the two groups began to build.

An American Indian chief and the governor of Virginia disagree during negotiations.

Some people think tensions rose because the colonists were too interested in profit. They searched for gold in the land, but they did not plant corn and other crops. They relied on the Powhatans for food. This became a problem.

The winter of 1608 was harsh. There were food shortages, so the Powhatans did not have enough food to trade. Colonists grew angry. They attacked the tribes and stole their food.

The colonists and the Powhatans were no longer **allies**. They became enemies. A series of wars began.

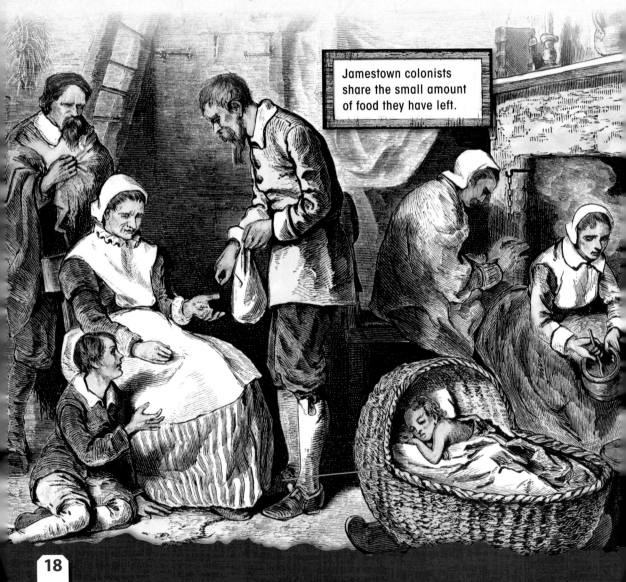

Jamestown colonists share the small amount of food they have left.

The **First Anglo-Powhatan War** started in 1609. The English wanted Chief Powhatan to serve the English king. This offended the Powhatans. The English kidnapped Pocahontas in 1610. In 1614, Pocahontas married a colonist named John Rolfe. Their marriage created peace between the two groups. But the peace did not last long. Pocahontas died just a few years later. Relations grew unstable again.

A second war started in 1622. It lasted for 10 years. A peace agreement ended it for a while. In 1644, a third war began. It lasted until the Powhatan leader was killed two years later.

Pocahontas marries John Rolfe.

Courageous Peacemaker

Some historians believe Pocahontas wanted to marry John Rolfe. Others think she did not have much choice. She had been held prisoner by the English for more than a year. She wanted peace for her people.

Taking Sides

Wars with settlers were not the only conflicts the Woodland People faced. They also fought in the colonial wars. The wars began in 1689. They were mainly between England and France. Both countries wanted to control North America. Colonists fought for their home countries. Tribes chose sides based on old feuds and alliances. Some chose based on their relations with the French and the English. Others chose based on what their enemies chose.

A tribe attacks a Massachusetts town.

These wars were broken by periods of uneasy peace. But the peace never lasted long, and the wars dragged on for years. Woodland People suffered and died in each of these wars. And the wars fueled more conflict among the tribes.

By His Excellency

Coll. *Benjamin Fletcher* Captain General and Governour in Chief of His Majesties Province of *New-York, &c.*

A PROCLAMATION

WHEREAS The *French* and *Indians* of *Canada* have lately Invaded the Country of the Indians of the Five Nations in Amity with the Subjects of the Crown of *England*, and have destroyed their Indian Corn. To the end that the said *Indians* that have so suffered the loss of their Corn, may be supplyed with what is necessary for their Maintenance for the Year ensuing, I have therefore, by and with the Advice and Consent of His Majesties Council for this Province, Prohibited the Transportation of Indian Corn and Pease from the County of *Albany*, *Ulster* and *Dutches County*, to any other County or Place down the River, until the first day of *April* now next ensuing. And all Masters of Sloops, and other Vessels are hereby prohibited accordingly, as they will answer the contrary at their peril.

Given at Fort William Henry the Twelfth Day of September, in the Eighth Year of the Reign of our Soveraign Lord WILLIAM the Third, by the Grace of God, King of England, Scotland, France and Ireland, Defender of the Faith, &c. Annoq; Domini 1696.

Ben. Fletcher.

God Save the KING

Printed by William Bradford, *Printer to the Kings most Excellent Majesty*, *at the Bible in the City of New-York*, 1696.

This proclamation from one of the colonial wars helped counties that were raided.

Five Nations

The Iroquois Confederacy was a powerful force among the American Indians. The alliance was formed between 1570 and 1600. It was made up of five tribes: the Onondaga, Cayuga, Mohawk, Seneca, and Oneida.

Iroquois Confederacy leaders meet to discuss laws.

21

The French and Indian War was the last of the colonial wars. It started in 1754 and ended in 1763. It was part of a larger war in Europe called the Seven Years' War. During the French and Indian War, Great Britain and France fought for control of the Ohio River Valley.

The British won the war. They punished tribes who fought for the French by cutting off their supplies. But the British did not really reward tribes who had fought with them. They tried to force all tribes to obey British law. And they stopped trading guns and gunpowder. British settlers took more tribal land after the war. Some tribes fought the British over land rights. So in 1763, the British **government** limited where colonists could settle.

Great Britain made new policies after the war. It wanted more control over its colonies. To pay off its war **debts**, Great Britain placed taxes on many things colonists used. Some colonists didn't feel loyal to Great Britain anymore. They felt loyal to their home in America.

a battle during the French and Indian War

British or English?

All the English can also be called British. But not all the British are English. Why? In 1707, Scotland joined England and Wales. Today, it also includes Northern Ireland. The country is called Great Britain or the United Kingdom.

Frustrated by new taxes, colonists throw tea into the Boston Harbor in 1773.

NORTH ATLANTIC OCEAN

NORTH SEA

SCOTLAND

Aberdeen

Dundee
Perth

Glasgow   Edinburgh
East
Kilbride

UNITED
KINGDOM

Carlisle   Sunderland

NORTHERN
IRELAND

Middlesbrough

Belfast

Isle of
Man
Douglas

York
Kingston upon Hull

IRELAND

Blackpool   Bradford   Leeds
Preston   Huddersfield
Bolton   Manchester
Liverpool   Sheffield

DUBLIN

IRISH SEA

ENGLAND

Stoke-   Derby
on-Trent   Nottingham

Wolverhampton   Leicester   Peterborough   Norwich
Birmingham   Northampton   Cambridge   Ipswich

WALES   Milton Keynes   Luton
Swansea   Gloucester   Swindon   LONDON   Southend-on-Sea
Newport   Bristol   Reading   Croydon   Dover
Cardiff   Bath   Winchester   Brighton   Hastings
Southampton   Portsmouth
Exeter   Poole
Plymouth

CELTIC SEA

ENGLISH CHANNEL

FRANCE

Guernsey

Many colonists felt they didn't need the British after the war. They were also unhappy about the new taxes. They wanted independence. They wanted to create their own country. In 1775, the colonists went to war again. But this time, they fought against Great Britain. This war became known as the American Revolution.

Many tribes joined the fight. Some fought for the Americans. They had shared land with them for many years. They had personal relationships with them. Other tribes fought for Great Britain. The British had promised to protect tribal land from new settlers.

The war ended in 1783. The colonists won. The United States of America had become its own country. But the new country betrayed and killed many of the tribes that helped them. They took land from tribes that fought both with and against them in the war. Many tribes of the East lost the land they had lived on for centuries.

In the years that followed, the Woodland People would face even more hardships. Many would be forced to leave their homes. But they always tried to hold onto their cultures.

British General John Burgoyne speaks to his American Indian allies before they attack a fort in 1777.

Tribes of the East Today

Many tribes of the East still exist. The largest tribes include the Cherokee, Choctaw, Chippewa, and Muscogee (Creek). Today, American Indians are free to live where they choose. They may live on **reservations**. There are over 300 federal reservations in the United States. They are much smaller than the land the tribes lived on long ago. But tribes can have their own governments on reservations.

Most American Indians today live in modern houses. They go to modern schools and wear modern clothing. Many tribes help their people with housing, job training, healthcare, and other issues.

Tribes also try to keep their cultures alive. People take part in festivals and ceremonies. They sing songs and wear traditional clothing. Some people teach language classes. Some teach traditional ways of cooking. Tribal members write books and give speeches to tell others about their unique cultures. They are proud of their **heritage**.

Many tribes attend this powwow in New York.

Cook It!

Create a cookbook of eastern American Indian recipes. Research traditional recipes online. Search for dishes that include the Three Sisters as ingredients. Try to find a mix of main courses, side dishes, breads, and desserts.

Print the recipes or write them on separate sheets of paper. Be sure to list the ingredients and the directions. Organize the recipes by type. Then, bind them to create a cookbook. Design a cover for your book. With adult permission, you might try making some of the dishes! You could even post pictures of your dishes online with adult help.

Three Sisters salad

Old-fashioned
RECIPE BOOK
SECRET FAMILY RECIPES FROM THE PAST

Glossary

alliances—relationships in which people agree to join together

allies—people who join together for a common cause or goal

ambush—the act of hiding, waiting for others to appear, and then suddenly attacking them

Anglo-Powhatan War—a series of three wars between the English and the Powhatans in the 1600s

captives—people who are captured and kept as prisoners

Christianity—a religion based on the belief in the teachings of Jesus Christ

colonists—people who live in an area that is ruled by another country

colony—an area ruled by a country far away

convert—to change from one religion or belief to another

cultures—the beliefs and ways of groups of people

customs—traditional behaviors or actions of a group of people

debts—amounts of money owed to someone

government—a group of leaders who make choices for a country or region

heritage—traditions and beliefs that are part of the history of a group or nation

manufactured—usually made in large amounts by using machines

profit—to have a financial gain

reservations—areas of land in the United States that are kept separate as places for American Indians to live

savages—brutal, rude, and uncivilized people

tribes—groups of people who have the same language, customs, and beliefs

wattle and daub—a type of building in which woven sticks are covered in clay

Index

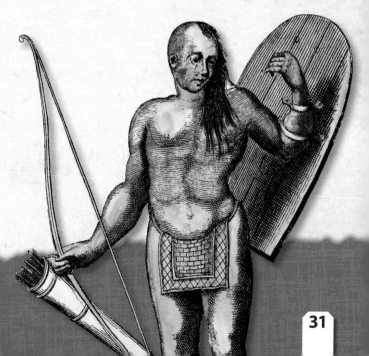

Your Turn!

Modern Powwows

Many tribes today attend inter-tribal powwows. These are gatherings where many tribes celebrate their cultures and traditions together. How might this help tribes preserve their cultures? How might this be similar to and different from inter-tribal relations long ago? Write a paragraph to answer these questions.